D1708042

ANIMAL SAFARI

Koalas

by Kari Schuetz

BELLWETHER MEDIA · MINNEAPOLIS, MN

Note to Librarians, Teachers, and Parents:

Blastoff! Readers are carefully developed by literacy experts and combine standards-based content with developmentally appropriate text.

Level 1 provides the most support through repetition of high-frequency words, light text, predictable sentence patterns, and strong visual support.

Level 2 offers early readers a bit more challenge through varied simple sentences, increased text load, and less repetition of high-frequency words.

Level 3 advances early-fluent readers toward fluency through increased text and concept load, less reliance on visuals, longer sentences, and more literary language.

Level 4 builds reading stamina by providing more text per page, increased use of punctuation, greater variation in sentence patterns, and increasingly challenging vocabulary.

Level 5 encourages children to move from "learning to read" to "reading to learn" by providing even more text, varied writing styles, and less familiar topics.

Whichever book is right for your reader, Blastoff! Readers are the perfect books to build confidence and encourage a love of reading that will last a lifetime!

This edition first published in 2012 by Bellwether Media, Inc.

No part of this publication may be reproduced in whole or in part without written permission of the publisher. For information regarding permission, write to Bellwether Media, Inc., Attention: Permissions Department, 5357 Penn Avenue South, Minneapolis, MN 55419.

Library of Congress Cataloging-in-Publication Data
Schuetz, Kari.
Koalas / by Kari Schuetz.
   p. cm. – (Blastoff! readers. animal safari)
Includes bibliographical references and index.
 Summary: "Developed by literacy experts for students in kindergarten through grade three, this book introduces koalas to young readers through leveled text and related photos"–Provided by publisher.
ISBN 978-1-60014-607-7 (hardcover : alk. paper)
 1. Koala–Juvenile literature. I. Title.
QL737.M384S39 2012
599.2'5–dc22   2011007192

Printed in the United States of America, North Mankato, MN.

080111   1187

Contents

What Are Koalas?

Koalas are **marsupials**. They have gray fur and black noses.

Where Koalas Live

Koalas live in **eucalyptus** forests. They spend most of their time asleep in trees.

Koalas use sharp **claws** to climb trees.

claws

Eating

Koalas eat eucalyptus leaves. These leaves are tough and thick.

Koalas **grind** the leaves with their teeth. They make a **paste** they can swallow.

Pouches and Joeys

A female koala
has a **pouch**
on her belly.
She carries her
baby in the pouch.

A newborn koala is the size of a jelly bean. It is called a joey.

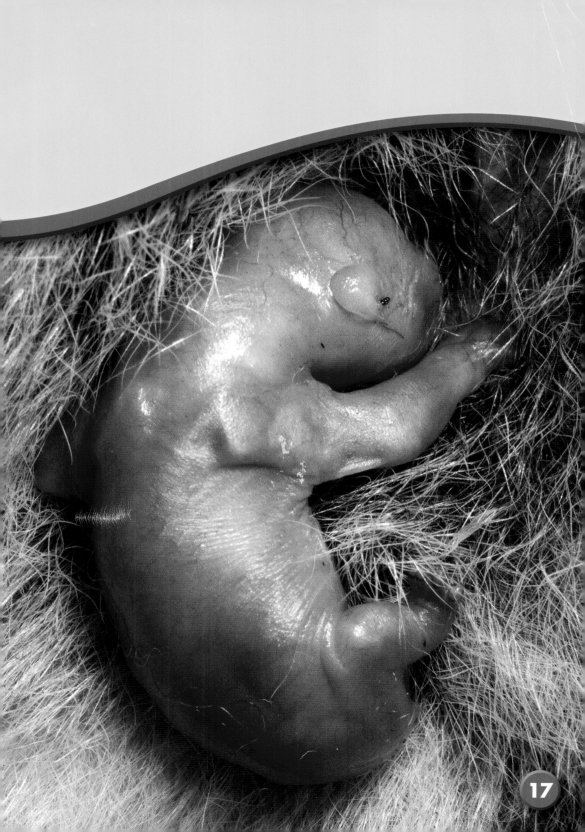

A joey stays
in its mother's
pouch for about
six months.

Then the joey
comes out.
It rides on its
mother's back.
Hold on joey!

Glossary

claws—sharp, curved nails on the feet of some animals

eucalyptus—woody plants that can be small bushes or large trees

grind—to wear down; koalas grind leaves with their teeth.

marsupials—animals that carry their babies in pouches

paste—a soft, smooth substance; koalas grind leaves into a paste they can swallow.

pouch—a pocket of skin on the belly of a female marsupial; marsupials use their pouches to carry their babies.

To Learn More

AT THE LIBRARY

Fox, Mem. *Koala Lou.* San Diego, Calif.: Harcourt Brace Jovanovich, 1988.

Hengel, Katherine. *It's a Baby Koala!* Edina, Minn.: ABDO, 2010.

Kras, Sara Louise. *Koalas.* Mankato, Minn.: Capstone Press, 2010.

ON THE WEB

Learning more about koalas is as easy as 1, 2, 3.

1. Go to www.factsurfer.com.

2. Enter "koalas" into the search box.

3. Click the "Surf" button and you will see a list of related Web sites.

With factsurfer.com, finding more information is just a click away.

Index

The images in this book are reproduced through the courtesy of: Eric Isselée, front cover; J & C Sohns / Photolibrary, pp. 5, 11; Andras Deak, p. 7; David Wall / Alamy, p. 9; Ronald Wittek / Age Fotostock, p. 13; Sam Yeh / Getty Images, p. 15; D. Parer & E. Parer-Cook / Minden Pictures, p. 17; Bruce Lichtenberger / Photolibrary, p. 19; Klein-Hubert / Kimballstock, p. 21.